GUIDELINES
for Leading Your Congregation

HIGHER EDUCATION AND CAMPUS MINISTRY

Connecting with students in schools, colleges, and campus ministries

Written by James A. Noseworthy and
Graham P. Matthews
General Board of Higher Education and Ministry

D1091719

HIGHER EDUCATION AND CAMPUS MINISTRY

Copyright © 2000 by Cokesbury

This book is printed on elemental-chlorine–free paper.

ISBN: 0-687-3547-3

MANUFACTURED IN THE UNITED STATES OF AMERICA

CONTENTS

Our Identity, Call, and Mission

About now a small voice in the back of your mind may be whispering, "What am I doing here? To what have I said yes? What is my role?" At the same time you may be aware that your congregation has extended to you a *call—a call to serve.* And you have said *yes—yes to leading in a vital mission.*

The mission of The United Methodist Church is to make disciples of Jesus Christ. You have agreed to serve as a leader bringing your unique passions, gifts, and abilities to the church. When the leaders focus on the church's purpose—*its mission of making disciples of Jesus Christ*—and link that purpose to the passions of the people, amazing things can happen.

The fundamental <u>way</u> we fulfill our mission is to reach out to people in the name of Jesus Christ, to relate people to God, to nurture and strengthen them in their journey of discipleship, and to send them into the world to be the church—inviting and receiving others in the name of Jesus Christ. We call this the primary task of The United Methodist Church. Effective leaders keep the whole of the primary task in their sight, working to keep all of its aspects in concert.

Leaders in the church must be first, and foremost, spiritual leaders who model and embrace Christian discipline and teaching. *By practicing the means of grace*—prayer, fasting, studying Scripture, corporate worship, celebration of the Lord's Supper, Christian conversation, and acts of mercy—*church leaders stay tuned to the mission of the church and live out the primary task.* Members and would-be members should be able to look to a congregation's leaders for spiritual example and direction, because true leaders are known by their fruits. People's lives are changed through their influence.

Leaders use their gifts and talents to enable others to use <u>their</u> gifts and talents to the fullest potential. The flow of information, inspiration, guidance, and vision from leaders is an encouragement to others on their spiritual journey. Leaders help others to see new possibilities. When leaders are focused on the mission of the church, community is built and ministry occurs. The church focused on God is alive with creative energy aimed at transformation.

Four Essential Leadership Functions

Church leaders support and strengthen the church when they pay attention to these leadership functions: *(1) help people discover the current* *reality in which they live; (2) bring together the congregation's understandings of <u>current</u> reality and <u>desired</u> reality into a shared vision; (3) develop the plans to help the community move from current reality toward the reality of its shared vision; and finally, (4) monitor the whole work of the church as the congregation moves with God's guidance toward its vision.*

1. Discovering Current Reality

Accurately describing current reality—the way things are—may be the most important function of leadership. The booklets in this Guideline series offer suggestions for leaders to pay attention to the various committees of the church's ministry. In addition, it is critical for church leaders—lay and clergy—to spend time together discussing the ministry of the <u>whole</u> congregation. The conversation needs to include attentiveness to God's guidance and everything that describes a congregation's "what we are, here and now." Because God is always doing a new thing, this job is continuous. When we pay attention to change, we provide a base of integrity and strength from which to move into the future. Faith in Jesus Christ and a spiritual centering in God offers the strongest foundation to move people fearlessly through the massive changes of the twenty-first century.

2. Naming Shared Vision

Ask the question, "What do you want more than anything else in the world?" and most persons will give a response that indicates that they want to live in a world filled with love, faith, security, and meaning. Because persons desire a positive future, they are willing to invest themselves in organizations that are committed to it. By its very nature, the church is devoted to the creation of a better future. When the church promises to move people personally and corporately toward their desired reality, people will invest time, energy, and resources into the church. As people see their own desires linked to the congregational vision and deeper understanding of God's future, they deepen their commitment and involvement. Building this link is a vital role of leadership.

Naming a shared vision is accomplished by asking people about their lives and their faith, and listening very carefully. By listening, we mean deep listening—the kind that requires setting aside our own agendas and entering into the worldviews of others, and listening for God through the conversation. It is a significant shift in our understanding of leadership in the church to move from telling people what we think they need to know to listening to people in order to find out who they are and what their desired realities are. Effective spiritual leaders listen to the hearts of people and begin to articulate a shared vision.

3. Developing Bridges

To span the gulf between our current reality and the hope expressed in the shared vision, leaders must build a bridge. The third critical function of leadership is to plan actions and develop systems that create the bridge across this gulf. Leaders who are elected to administrative and program committees are responsible for the ongoing work of the church and must pay attention to the present. At the same time, leaders *must* be focused on the future—keeping today and tomorrow in tension—ensuring that the church doesn't get stuck in the past, present, or future.

Church leaders who are attentive to God's leading and who can hold the tension between today and tomorrow are *visionary leaders*. Visionary leaders see it all—current reality, desired reality, and the bridges to get from one to the other.

4. Monitoring the Journey

Perhaps the most critical task for leaders is keeping an eye on the whole of the faith journey of the congregation. When leaders are constantly caught up in "doing" the administrative and program work of the church, there is not any time left for "being" with God in prayer to discern the leading of the Spirit for the congregation. Leaders must step back from "doing" constant activities in order to pay attention to the total direction of the church's mission and ministry. All elected and appointed leaders must spend time together listening to God in prayer, Bible study, conversation, and other means of grace in order to lead the entire community in the work of Christ. Anything less is not Christian spiritual leadership.

This Is Your Ministry!

Thank you for assuming leadership for a special ministry of your church: higher education and campus ministry. The college years are a time when students shape the dreams and visions that will influence the rest of their lives. Those years also are a time when students examine the faith and values that will support their life choices. Your ministry helps students know that the church affirms them as they increase in knowledge and shape those visions. That is no small responsibility!

The responsibility is not yours alone; it is for a team of individuals working together to advocate for the church's ministry in higher education. You are the team leader for your congregation. Gather a team of individual workers to join you. In large churches, a committee may have been appointed to work with you; in small churches, you may be the only one officially designated with responsibility for higher education and campus ministry. **Invite people to join the team: parents, teachers, students, and high school guidance counselors.**

New responsibilities can seem overwhelming. The following information will assist you in understanding the scope of your work and will provide some practical resources for fulfilling your responsibilities.

As chair of the ministry team of higher education and campus ministry, you will need to recruit other laypersons to assist you with these responsibilities:
- keeping the council on ministries or church council aware of higher education and campus ministry concerns;
- promoting local church support for the higher education and campus ministry programs of the annual conference and of the Division of Higher Education of the General Board of Higher Education and Ministry;
- interpreting and promoting the Black College Fund and the Hispanic, Asian, and Native American (HANA) educational ministries;
- recruiting students for United Methodist-related colleges and encouraging students to participate in United Methodist campus ministry units;
- planning your church's ministry to and with college and university students, staff, faculty, and administrators in the local church;
- encouraging local support of United Methodist-related colleges, universities, and campus ministries in the annual conference;
- relating students to United Methodist-supported campus ministries;
- promoting the United Methodist Student Loan and Scholarship Funds through the observance of United Methodist Student Day and World Communion Sunday offerings;
- alerting the pastor, parents, and students to the availability of loans and scholarships for United Methodist students through the Office of Loans and Scholarships of the General Board of Higher Education and Ministry, the United Methodist Foundation for Christian Higher Education, the annual conference, and the local church.

Elected by the charge conference for a one-year term, you are a member of the council on ministries or the church council, and the charge conference. You are responsible for interpreting and recommending to the church council ways for implementing the church's mission in higher education and campus ministry. You work with the guidance of the pastor and the chairperson of the church council.

Several resources for your work are listed in this guide. They include information about the history of United Methodism, the educational ministries, interpretation of programs in the area of higher education ministries, a sample calendar of a year's program, and printed, video, and personal resources.

A resource that will be especially valuable is *Interpreter* magazine, a monthly program journal for local church leaders. Several copies are sent free to each church; additional subscriptions are available at a nominal cost. Order from United Methodist Communications, P.O. Box 320, 810 Twelfth Avenue South, Nashville, TN 37202-0320.

Resources and information regarding United Methodist higher education ministries can be found on the Internet. The main address is http://www.gbhem.org. From there, you can go to specific pages about higher education issues and resources.

The staff of the Office of Annual Conference Relations of the Division of Higher Education is available to answer questions and discuss issues. The mail address is P.O. Box 340007, Nashville, TN 37203-0007; telephone: 615-340-7402; e-mail: gmatthews@gbhem.org. A directory of information available on the Internet can be found on pages 31 and 32.

Now What Do I Do?

One place to begin understanding your congregation's ministry in higher education is to recognize each local church's responsibility for "planning and implementing a program of nurture, outreach, and witness for persons and families within and without the congregation" (*Discipline* ¶ 242). Within and beyond your congregation, you find individuals who are on the college campus and engaged in higher education. You and your church have the opportunity to develop creative ministries of nurture, outreach, and witness with and for these persons!

A strong program in higher education and campus ministry in your church must have the understanding and support of key persons. It is important to consult with your pastor and the chairperson of the church council. In a small church, one person may well be able to manage this ministry area. In middle-size churches, task forces could help in planning and promoting special events. In larger churches, a standing commission might be in order. Even then, special events for students who are home from college may call for subcommittees or task forces. The way you organize your work will affect all that you do. As you read this guide, make notes to help you choose the best approach for accomplishing your tasks. Most important, think about the best way to minister to persons in higher education. Then put your plans and ideas to work! Here are some ways to begin.

1. ***Request resource materials*** *from the Office of Annual Conference Relations, Division of Higher Education, General Board of Higher Education and Ministry.* You may contact the office by phone: 615-340-7402; by mail: P.O. Box 340007, Nashville, TN 37203-0007; or by

e-mail: gmatthews@gbhem.org. A list of all United Methodist-related schools, colleges, and universities, and a directory of all United Methodist-related campus ministries, along with other resources, are available from the Division of Higher Education.

2. *Identify your constituents:*
   - High school juniors and seniors as potential candidates for United Methodist-related colleges, universities, and campus ministries
   - Students now at college, both undergraduate and graduate level
   - High school counselors who assist students in their college planning
   - College administrators, faculty, and staff members and trustees who are related to your church
   - College chaplains and campus ministers
   - Commuting students in your congregation

3. *Read* Interpreter *magazine.* Check the regular columns on higher education and campus ministry in the "Idea Mart" section for ideas to use in the local church.

4. *Talk with others in the congregation about ministry in higher education.* Learn of their concerns for students, staff, and faculty at colleges. What are their ideas for making your local church's ministry in higher education an important and creative part of the lives of those who are studying, teaching, or working at colleges and universities? Perhaps there are people in your local church who would covenant to pray regularly for this ministry that God might lead your church to be involved in ministry in higher education in new ways.

On pages 21 to 24 you will find the section "Some Ideas for Action." Read it, and add ideas of your own.

Learning More About Higher Education Ministries in Your Area

Help members of your congregation become better informed about what is happening on campus. Organize a Sunday night supper and discussion introducing members of the church family to some key people in higher education ministries. Invite a college student, a faculty member, a local campus ministry board member, an administrator, and a campus minister or chaplain to be part of the program and discussion. Let each person describe for the group what it is like to be involved in college life today.

Questions you might ask participants include:

1. *A college student*—
   a. Why are you in college? What led you to choose your particular college?
   b. Where do you live, and what else do you do besides go to school?

   c. Do you participate in any campus activities?

2. *A faculty member at a college or university*—
   a. How would you describe your campus (size, public or private, its mission)?
   b. What subject(s) do you teach?
   c. What, in your opinion, are the three most pressing issues on college campuses today?

   d. How does your religious faith influence what you do in education?

3. *A local campus ministry board member*—
   a. What is your occupation?
   b. Why do you think the church should be involved in ministry in higher education?
   c. What three specific programs would you like to see the campus minister do?

4. *A campus minister or college chaplain*—
   a. How long have you been at this campus ministry?
   b. What special training or preparation did you have for this job?

   c. What do you most enjoy about being a campus minister or college chaplain?

   d. What is your relationship to the churches that sponsor your ministry?
   e. What connections do you maintain between your campus ministry and local churches? With regional and state organizations?
   f. What, in your opinion, are the three most pressing issues on college campuses today?
   g. How is your campus ministry or college chaplaincy addressing those issues?

After each participant has made a presentation, invite the congregation to ask questions. Encourage discussion. At the end of the evening, ask two or three people to share with the group some insights and understandings. What might these understandings mean for your church's ministry in higher education?

Why Should the Church be Involved in Higher Education?

Every United Methodist in this country feels the impact of higher education. Like the air we breathe, it penetrates everything—and touches everyone.

College is a time and place where people ask hard questions: Who am I? Who am I called to be? What should I do with my life? What is true? What is false? College includes a search for knowledge, for beauty, for a vision of what the world could be. Almost every major decision in our country is made by graduates of colleges and universities. Most of the businesses and corporations of our nation and world are staffed and led by college graduates. Most pastors must graduate both college and seminary.

We're involved in higher education because more and more of our neighbors and our church family go to college. Approximately 14.5 million persons are enrolled in some kind of post–high school education in the United States. Approximately 28 percent of college students in the United States are thirty years of age or older. Most older students live at home and commute to school. They are among us. You may be one of them.

We're not only affected by higher education; we have a stake in it. If colleges train our community's, nation's, and world's decision makers, we need to build Christian and humane values into those decisions. The church is called to witness to the love, compassion, and concern of God on the campus. The church must witness to the relation of faith to knowledge, and to the direct relationship between the intellectual and the moral.

A student body may have large numbers of single parents, women preparing to enter the job market for the first time, persons with disabilities, newly unemployed persons, workers needing additional skills in order to keep their jobs, people who have found their present lives unfulfilling and who wish to explore new possibilities.

The pathway to success often goes through college. For some ethnic persons in the U.S., that path has often been blocked by poverty or prejudice. As they begin the transition from prejudice to empowerment, ethnic persons turn to higher education.

Our concern for people brings United Methodists into ministry in higher education. The United Methodist Church continues a 250-year tradition of ministry in education. John Wesley began the Holy Club and the Methodist Society with a student at Kings College, Oxford University. Wesley was a tireless reader, writer, translator, and book and pamphlet publisher. He also founded the Kingswood School, the first Methodist educational institution in England.

When The Methodist Church began in the United States in 1784, one of its first acts was the creation of Cokesbury College. Members of The Evangelical United Brethren tradition were equally zealous educators, as the presence of Otterbein and Albright Colleges testifies. People of the Methodist tradition were challenged to bring educational opportunity to the frontier; as a result, the people established approximately one thousand schools across the North American continent. In 1913, the first Wesley Foundation was founded on the campus of the University of Illinois.

One hundred twenty-three schools, colleges, universities, seminaries, and professional schools and more than seven hundred campus ministry units are related to The United Methodist Church. These colleges and campus ministries represent the church's care and concern for people; they express the church's concern for learning, love, and enlightenment to take root and flourish in higher education.

United Methodists are organized to keep our involvement in higher education fresh and vital. In every local congregation, a person is selected to coordinate a program in ministry in higher education. Every annual conference has a Board of Higher Education and Campus Ministry or equivalent structure to help local churches do their work and to work directly with schools, colleges, and campus ministries. The Division of Higher Education of the General Board of Higher Education and Ministry coordinates and enlivens the denomination's mission in higher education nationally and internationally.

The church is involved in higher education—faithful people grooming faithful minds for faithful lives.

United Methodist Themes in Higher Education

Church-Related Colleges, Universities, and Secondary Schools

The United Methodist Church has a long and impressive history in higher learning. Since the founding of Cokesbury College in 1784, hundreds of institutions have been founded by United Methodists in the United States. That heritage continues today in the sponsorship of 10 major research universities, 13 seminaries, 82 liberal arts colleges, 8 two-year colleges, 1 professional school, and 9 college preparatory schools. The following map will help you locate them.

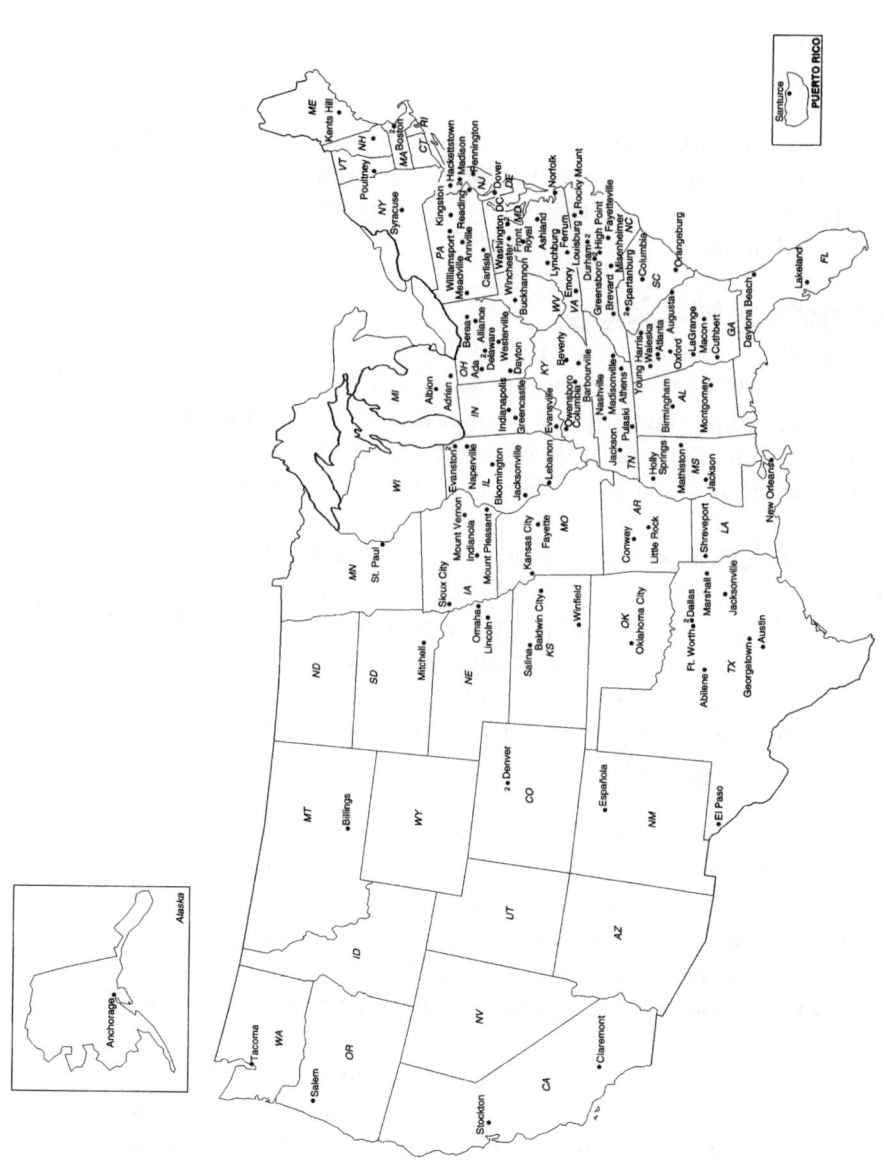

Our involvement in higher education reflects the social concerns of The United Methodist Church. Several institutions were founded especially for women, and others for blacks, during a time when it was neither popular nor widely expected that women and blacks should have educational opportunities.

There are now 4 colleges for women and 11 historically black colleges related to The United Methodist Church. Overall, the church has had historic ties with more than 1,000 institutions. The number of institutions currently in the family gives United Methodism the largest Protestant presence in higher education in the nation. The variety of institutions has contributed significantly to student access, equity, and democracy in higher education in the United States.

Campus Ministry

United Methodist campus ministry is diverse, taking many forms and offering different programs at approximately 700 locations in the U.S. United Methodist campus ministry is versatile. It takes many forms in many places; it offers different programs for different people. When knowledge and vital piety fuse, ministry happens. Campus ministry illustrates that.

United Methodists sponsor campus ministry in at least four ways. First, we have Wesley Foundations—United Methodist campus ministry centers—on some publicly supported and independent college campuses. Second, we have ecumenical units—those we support together with other denominations—on other campuses. Third, college chaplains minister at our church-related colleges. Finally, many local congregations now extend their ministries to embrace nearby colleges.

What happens in campus ministry includes what happens in other ministries: worship, Bible study, singing, service projects, counseling, classes, convocations, and community events. Much time is spent with students. However, as student populations become older and their needs change, the ministry with and to them also changes. Groups for singles, child-care facilities, and fellowship groups for foreign students are just a few new wrinkles in campus ministry.

Campus ministry continues to expand its radius of concern. Faculty, staff, and administrators are the most stable parts of the campus population. Often, working through them, campus ministry is able to reach many more people. For example, through their friendship with college personnel, campus ministers have been able to draw them into unique programs: teachers of engineering helping to rehabilitate poor housing; medical educators working with the poor in our country and others; law students and faculty lending their services to persons who cannot afford legal counsel.

From student movements to faculty study, from prayer breakfasts to social service, from personal counseling to global concerns, campus ministry embodies the church's mission to the world.

The Black College Fund

Through the Black College Fund, United Methodists continue their significant and long-standing tradition of providing educational opportunities to an important segment of the U.S. population. For more than a century, even before the Emancipation Proclamation, Methodists were in the forefront of the movement to improve the quality of life for black men and women.

In 1872, the Freedmen's Aid Society was formed; thirty-four colleges, academies, and theological schools were founded in the first fifty years of the society's existence. Often starting as small schoolrooms, these institutions grew to become established undergraduate colleges and universities located primarily in the South.

Eleven of these colleges continue as historically black institutions related to The United Methodist Church: Bennett College (Greensboro, North Carolina); Bethune-Cookman College (Daytona Beach, Florida); Claflin University (Orangeburg, South Carolina); Clark Atlanta University (Atlanta, Georgia); Dillard University (New Orleans, Louisiana); Huston-Tillotson College (Austin, Texas); Meharry Medical College (Nashville, Tennessee); Paine College (Augusta, Georgia); Philander Smith College (Little Rock, Arkansas); Rust College (Holly Springs, Mississippi); and Wiley College (Marshall, Texas).

Contributions for black education were made by churches and individuals within The Methodist Episcopal Church. Because of the great financial need, the Board of Managers of the Freedmen's Aid Society sought and received General Conference approval as a benevolent agency in 1872. Since then, the church has supported the black colleges through a series of special day observances and celebrations. In 1972, the General Conference of The United Methodist Church established the Black College Fund as one of the apportioned general church funds.

The colleges supported by the fund provide direct access, nurture, and professional and spiritual training and guidance to a student population that, in the main, would remain unserved without them.

The black colleges historically related to The United Methodist Church perform a very special kind of service. Enrollment continues to increase at these schools, with the institutions having a collective enrollment of 15,000 students per year.

Thanks to The United Methodist Church's historic commitment through the Black College Fund, educational access and academic and professional accomplishments continue to become realities for thousands of students of promise.

Hispanic, Asian, and Native American (HANA) Educational Ministries

The 1976 General Conference of The United Methodist Church created HANA—a fund to increase higher education opportunities for Hispanics, Asians, and Native Americans. HANA puts into action John Wesley's belief that education is for all people. The program helps to remedy long-standing inequities in access to higher education. As a result, many more leaders for The United Methodist Church and for American society have been nurtured.

Because leadership often requires advanced and professional education, the HANA scholarships target college juniors, seniors, and graduate students. More than one thousand students have benefited from this program and now are assuming leadership in the fields of business and industry, education, medicine, law, and the church. Annually, $500,000 is awarded to approximately two hundred graduate and seventy undergraduate students.

Because of increasing educational costs and the continuing decline of available financial aid, these scholarships are becoming even more crucial. Local congregations can work with the annual conference Board of Higher Education and Campus Ministry or equivalent structure, United Methodist colleges and theological schools, as well as with campus ministry units, to identify potential candidates for the scholarships and potential leaders for tomorrow. Local congregations can play an important role in interpreting and promoting this significant program of the church.

Global Higher Education

In the eighteenth and nineteenth centuries, United Methodists expressed their concern for the education of all persons by founding educational institutions throughout the world. During the past century, those institutions have become their nations' leading schools while maintaining a distinctive Christian character and tradition. The missionaries and educators hoped these institutions would join those in the U.S. and in other parts of the world to make a greater contribution to the human community.

The 1984 General Conference mandated the General Board of Higher Education and Ministry "to develop and maintain cooperative relationships with higher educational institutions, campus ministries, chaplains and related ministries, and diaconal ministries throughout the world." In collaboration with the General Board of Global Ministries and with other denominations, the General Board of Higher Education and Ministry is actively engaged in work in the international arena.

In 1991, the World Methodist Council established an Education Committee to further the council's involvement in issues relating to Christian value-centered education. During the same meeting, the International Association of Methodist-related Schools, Colleges, and Universities (IAMSCU) was created. The association links Methodist-related institutions throughout the world to promote the development of quality and value-centered education. The last meeting of IAMSCU was held in England in July 1998.

One result of efforts in international education is increased opportunities for faculty and student exchanges, constructive dialogues and conferences, and technical assistance.

Africa University

In 1992, the first students enrolled in Africa University. Located in Old Mutare, Zimbabwe, this initiative of the church established a church-related university in sub-Saharan Africa. The university was developed as a response to calls for leaders by the United Methodist Central Conferences in Africa.

Africa University, a university of international quality, currently has programs in theology, agriculture and natural resources, business administration, education, and humanities and social sciences. Approximately eight hundred students were enrolled in the university in August 2000.

For information about how you and your church might become involved in this important work, contact your pastor or the Africa University Development Office, P.O. Box 340007, Nashville, TN 37203-0007; telephone: 615-340-7438. Publications and videotapes to interpret this church-wide effort are available.

Office of Loans and Scholarships

The United Methodist Church Student Loan Program is the oldest and largest church program of its type in America. This program has been serving students in higher education for more than a century. Since the first Children's Offering in 1866, more than one-half million students have realized their vocational dreams with financial assistance from the United Methodist Student Loan and Scholarship Programs. The program made its first loan in 1872 to a student preparing for a lay vocation.

Personal testimonies from thousands of former recipients of a United Methodist student loan or scholarship reaffirm how vital the church's investment has been in their lives through this aspect of ministry.

The loan program operates as a revolving fund. As recipients repay their loans, the money is lent to other United Methodist students who are enrolled in degree programs at accredited institutions and who have a grade average of at least a C. The loan fund has a remarkable repayment rate of 99.5 percent.

The United Methodist Scholarship Program is a churchwide educational service providing scholarships to supplement the financial needs of today's students. Funding for these scholarships is provided through offerings, wills, annuities, and other designated gifts.

Scholarships are awarded on an academic-year basis. A student is eligible to receive only one scholarship from General Board of Higher Education and Ministry funds during any one academic year. All scholarship applicants must be full, active members of The United Methodist Church for at least one year prior to applying and must be attending an accredited educational institution in the United States.

> Be sure to observe United Methodist Student Day with an offering. Observed annually, this offering is the primary source of funds for loans and scholarships. Ten percent of the Student Day offering receipts are rebated annually by the Office of Loans and Scholarships to annual conferences participating in the Conference Merit Award Program.

Thirty-five percent of the World Communion Sunday offering supports the Ethnic Minority Scholarship Fund. A portion of the offering receipts from Native American Awareness Sunday provides scholarships to Native American United Methodist students pursuing a degree at a University Senate–approved school of theology.

Your students can apply for a loan or a scholarship by contacting the Office of Loans and Scholarships, P.O. Box 340007, Nashville, TN 37203; telephone: 615-340-7342; or visit our web site at www.gbhem.org.

The United Methodist Foundation for Christian Higher Education

The United Methodist Foundation for Christian Higher Education is an organization established under the provisions of *The Book of Discipline of The United Methodist Church* (¶ 1422). Its purpose is to raise, manage, and distribute funds to foster education in a Christian context in schools, colleges, universities, and theological schools within The United Methodist Church.

Since its founding in 1964, the foundation's assets have grown to almost $40 million. Its scholarship programs also have grown; awards totaling more than $4 million have been made. The foundation receives no money from the denomination.

The foundation is committed to furthering educational opportunity in several ways:

1. *Foundation Scholars:* A $1,000 scholarship **each** for a freshman, sophomore, and senior (four-year colleges and college preparatory schools) and for a freshman and sophomore (two-year colleges) at **each** of the United Methodist-related schools, colleges, and universities; and a $3,000 scholarship **each** for a first-, second-, and third-year student at **each** of the United Methodist-related theological and professional schools.
2. *Named Scholarships:* A program for annual conferences, districts, local churches, groups, and individuals to establish a scholarship in honor or memory of a person. The funds, invested through the foundation, are used to award a scholarship to an individual meeting the criteria established by the donors.
3. *Double Your Dollars for Scholars:* A $1,000 matching scholarship will be awarded to the first eligible 220 applicants, on a first-come, first-served basis. **The sponsoring church** must remit a check payable to UMFCHE for $1,000 with the completed application form.
4. *The Stanley Kresge Award:* An award recognizing a United Methodist individual's commitment to the church and to United Methodist-related education. A $10,000 scholarship is awarded to the educational institution where the recipient is a volunteer.
5. *Outstanding Educator Award:* An annual award honoring an individual whose teaching accomplishments have made an extraordinary impact on one's institution and one's students. The recipient receives a cash award of $5,000.
6. *Chaplain of the Year Award:* An annual award to the chaplain of a United Methodist-related college or university whose ministry is recognized as extraordinary. The $5,000 prize is to be used for the further development of the programs sponsored by the chaplain's office.
7. *Campus Minister of the Year Award:* Recognizes and encourages excellence in campus ministry. Each year the foundation selects one United Methodist campus minister serving in a Wesley Foundation or an ecumenical campus ministry for this award. The recipient receives a cash award of $5,000 to further the development of programs sponsored by the campus minister's office.

The foundation also assists in estate planning in relation to support of United Methodist Christian higher education.

For additional information about the foundation and its programs, write The United Methodist Foundation for Christian Higher Education, 1001 Nineteenth Avenue South, P.O. Box 340005, Nashville, TN 37203-0005; telephone: 615-340-7385, or visit their Web site at ww.umfche.org.

Education: The Gift of Hope

Reflecting the United Methodist concern for education, the 1996 General Conference received and recommended that churches a study the revised edition of *Education: The Gift of Hope*.

Created by a special committee coordinated by the General Board of Higher Education and Ministry, *Education: The Gift of Hope* (Revised) is a resource for every congregation to use in studying the issues concerning education in the U.S. The document reviews the current educational scene and challenges local congregations to become involved in meeting the educational needs of their communities.

For information about *Education: The Gift of Hope,* contact the Office of Annual Conference Relations, Division of Higher Education, P.O. Box 340007, Nashville, TN 37203-0007; telephone: 615-340-7402. Or order from Cokesbury; telephone: 800-672-1789; fax: 800-445-8189; order number 792047.

Higher Education and Campus Ministry in Your Local Church

Higher education can be an exciting expression of your congregation's ministry. It will be important for you to keep the concerns of higher education ministries before your church council and to integrate them into the program life of your church.

Interpret higher education ministries by personalizing them. As you describe programs, institutions, and causes, cite persons in your own congregation who have been affected by them. Also, become acquainted with your constituents. Some members of your congregation may work for or be graduates of United Methodist schools and colleges, serve on their boards, or be members of the board of directors of a campus ministry unit. You may have members of your district or annual conference Board of Higher Education and Campus Ministry or equivalent structure in your vicinity. And, of course, you may have students in your congregation, some of whom worship with you, and others who attend school away from home.

Meet with those individuals. Listen to them tell about their work. Share their stories with the congregation, and invite them to talk with others. What you learn from them will be helpful information for forming your program.

Some Ideas for Action

The following sections offer some ideas for ways to begin your ministry. Review them carefully, add your own ideas, and develop a program for the entire year. A suggested calendar of activities follows this material. You can also assist your local campus ministry by having your church start a non-profit foundation.

Make the Link Between the Local Church and Higher Education

1. Request materials from the Division of Higher Education (see the Resources section) for college-bound students. They should include copies of *College Bound,* loan and scholarship information, maps and directories that locate United Methodist colleges and universities, information on the historically black colleges, and the *Handbook of United Methodist-Related Schools, Colleges, Universities, and Theological Schools.*

2. Send names and addresses of high school sophomores and juniors in your church to United Methodist colleges and universities in or near your conference each spring.

3. Encourage prospective students to visit United Methodist colleges and universities. In the spring of their junior year or early in their senior year, organize a small group of students to visit one of the colleges. Contact the admissions director at least three weeks in advance to make arrangements for the visit.
4. Contact high school guidance counselors to be sure that they have up-to-date catalogs or admissions CD's of United Methodist colleges and universities.
5. Invite campus ministers and chaplains to lead the programs for youth groups.
6. Purchase *Orientation* magazine for students who will start college in the fall. Use it as a resource for a youth Sunday school class or for a student/parent study group. *Orientation* is available for order from the Campus Ministry Section of the General Board of Higher Education and Ministry.
7. Hold a recognition service for persons in your church connected with higher education. Include those graduating from high school as well as college students, administrators, faculty, staff members, and trustees. Refer to *Orientation* magazine for ideas and themes.

8. Give students information about loans and scholarships from GBHEM Office of Loans and Scholarships.
9. Submit the name of a qualified candidate to your annual conference Merit Scholarship Program. For specific information and the guidelines for these awards, check with the chairperson of your annual conference Board of Higher Education and Campus Ministry or equivalent structure.
10. Consider making a covenant with a local campus ministry unit or United Methodist college. This covenant would be a pledge between the local church and campus ministry or college to be supportive of one another's ministry. Samples of such covenants are available from the Division of Higher Education, General Board of Higher Education and Ministry in Nashville.

How to Keep in Touch with College Students Away from Home

1. Send the names of all college students, including commuting and part-time students, to the Wesley Foundation director, campus minister, or college chaplain at the school they attend. Do this early in the summer to give the campus pastor time to correspond with the students before school starts. The chairperson of your annual conference Board of Higher Education and Campus Ministry or equivalent structure should have a copy of the *Directory of Ministries in Higher Education* for the entire country. (See the Resources section for information on how to obtain your own copy.)
2. Develop a plan to keep in touch with your congregation's college students. Assign one student to a family by drawing names, and ask that family to keep in touch throughout the year. Special notes, "goody" boxes, care packages, news from home, contact with the student's parents—all these are gifts that a family of friends-in-faith could give to a student away from home, in the name of the entire congregation.
3. Send college students your church's newsletter and/or a collection once a month of worship bulletins. This is an easy and priceless contact.
4. Send a personal greeting to each student in your congregation who is away at college on his or her birthday and on the yearly baptism anniversary.
5. Plan celebrations and gatherings when students are home—breaks, summertime, Christmas holidays. Publicize these as times for students to gather over a free dinner or munchies to catch up on news of one another. Include students in the planning of the event.
6. Involve students in worship leadership when they are home on a visit. Greet them in church so that the congregation recognizes them. Make them feel as though they still have a place in their home church.
7. Establish a job pool for college students for summer and part-time holiday

jobs. Contact people in the congregation and in the community for job opportunities, and make these known to college students related to your church.

Make Contact with College Students in the Area

Here are some of the ways your congregation can be in ministry with students attending colleges (commuter, community, two-year, or four-year) or universities in your geographic area:

1. Let college students know what's going on at your church. Make them feel welcome when they attend worship. A creative ad campaign in the campus or town newspaper geared toward students could let students know your church's doors are open to them. (For example: Church shopping? We invite you to visit Peoples United Methodist Church for our 11:00 A.M. Sunday worship service. We are located at ...)
2. If you have a gym, offer an open gym night for students. Offer use of the church for student groups to meet, free of charge. During midterm and final exam times, open the church—for a quiet place to study, for brownies and snacks during study breaks, for prayer and meditation time.
3. Invite faculty and staff recommended by students to a "Meet and Eat" night—dinner and discussion about some topic of interest to students.
4. Welcome college students to worship with cookies. Giving them a dozen cookies to take back to the residence hall is a good reminder of the church's concern and love.
5. Invite international students to help you plan an ethnic dinner and celebration for the local church. Follow dinner with discussions about customs in the students' home countries.
6. Check with the campus minister or student affairs officer to find out the students' needs that your church could assist in meeting. On many campuses there is a great need among students for child care. Sometimes commuter students need a place to rest and study between classes.
7. Sponsor a "getting away from it all" weekend. Link students with families who have winter cabins or summer lake homes, or who would offer two nights of living in a real home and getting out of the dorm or apartment.
8. Encourage your pastor and the local campus minister to set up person-to-person programs. Adopt-a-Family, Adopt-a-Student, and Adopt-a-Grandparent programs allow students and church members to interact.

Make Contact with the Campus for Resources

Whether or not your local church is near a campus, you can draw on the resources of higher education to enhance the life of the church.

1. Invite campus ministers or college chaplains to bring musical groups, drama groups, or mime troops to perform in your church.
2. Approach faculty and staff at local colleges about doing workshops in teacher training, managing volunteers, family life education, religious history, art and architecture, financial management, computers, and so forth.
3. Ask college faculty, staff, and campus ministers to help address community and congregational problems, such as business ethics, politics and government, faith and technology, prison reform, and health care.
4. Use college library and audiovisual resources for programming in the local church.
5. Invite local campus ministers, college faculty, and staff to teach Sunday school classes, to preach in worship, and to lead special Lenten or Advent studies.
6. Ask college admissions and counseling personnel to meet with high school students, church members who are considering returning to school, and those who need vocational counseling.
7. Request program resources. Share your current concerns and program needs with campus ministers and college administrators; often they will know someone on campus who may be able to meet those needs.

Make Contact with the Campus for Understanding

You also can draw your church into closer relationship with higher education concerns by offering opportunities for church members to interact with people from college campuses.

1. Encourage church members of all ages to attend special events and activities held on campus for the community. Include announcements of these in church bulletins and newsletters.

2. Conduct a "college weekend" for church members who often don't have contact with the campus. Arrange with a college in your area to host church members on campus for a weekend. Invite them to live in the residence halls (if it is a residential college) and engage in programmed and unprogrammed conversation with students, staff, and faculty. The purpose is to provide an in-depth, though brief, study of life on a college campus. You might also want to take a group to a community college to compare and contrast the two settings.

3. Create interpretive programs about ministry in higher education that can be used in Sunday school classes, for programs with United Methodist Men and United Methodist Women, and for church forum programs. Campus ministers, college chaplains, and administrators at colleges are good resource persons for these programs.

Walking Through the Year

A Sample Calendar of Activity

Resources mentioned are more fully described in the Resources section.

August	☞ Gather the names of students from your congregation who will be attending college and university this year. ☞ Send first-year college students a copy of *Orientation* magazine.
September	☞ Obtain the college address for each student away. Place students on the mailing list for the church newsletter. ☞ Send the brochure *So . . . What About God Now That You're Off to College?* along with a note from you or your ministry team to all students from your church. ☞ Present information about Africa University to the congregation. ☞ Invite a United Methodist college or campus ministry unit to present a program at your church in November or at another time during the year. ☞ Create a bulletin board with the names and pictures of members of your congregation attending college—and a map giving the locations of their schools. ☞ Present information about the Crusade Scholarship Program, the Ethnic Minority Scholarship Program, and Ethnic In-Service Training Program to the congregation (all are supported by the World Communion Day offering).
October	☞ Send students a copy of *Singing the Songs of Zion in a Strange New Land.* ☞ Prepare for observing United Methodist Student Day in November; visit with your pastor concerning ways to

	interpret the United Methodist Student Loan and Scholarship Programs. (Obtain offering envelopes and interpretive materials from United Methodist Communications.) ☞ Coordinate a visit by your church's high school youth to a nearby United Methodist college or campus ministry (many colleges plan a student day in the fall). ☞ List the names and addresses of your students in the church newsletter; invite parishioners to make contact with them.
November	☞ Promote the Student Day offering. ☞ Share information and stories about how the United Methodist Student Loan and Scholarship Programs have benefited present and former students from your congregation. ☞ Send a copy of the campus ministry Advent meditation booklet to college students. ☞ Host a program by the students at a United Methodist college or campus ministry unit. ☞ Coordinate a study group during the church school hour or at another time on the church's concern for ministry in higher education. Use the resource *Education: The Gift of Hope,* a study of education in the United States and how every congregation can be involved in educational concerns. Invite area leaders in higher education to speak about issues in higher education.
December	☞ Host a gathering for the church's college students during the Christmas holidays.
January	☞ Host a college night for your congregation and other churches to introduce students and families to United Methodist colleges and universities—and United Methodist financial aid options; contact an area United Methodist college for leadership.

	☞ Develop a display about United Methodist ministries in higher education for your church; include brochures and pictures about colleges and about campus ministries.
February	☞ Promote the Black College Fund and the mission of the historically black colleges related to The United Methodist Church. Send a midterm letter of encouragement to students; include a copy of the Lenten meditation booklet.
March	☞ In cooperation with your pastor, invite a college president, college chaplain, or campus minister to speak in a worship service about the United Methodist ministry in higher education; invite the guest to visit with a church school class, too. ☞ Contact the chair of your annual conference Board of Higher Education and Campus Ministry or equivalent structure to host a Black College Fund intern for an event during June or July.
April	☞ Request newsletters and publicity items about religious programs on campus from college chaplains and campus ministers; create a display for the church.
May	☞ Send congratulatory letters to students graduating from college and to students graduating from high school. ☞ Create a display board with pictures of the graduates and words about their future plans. ☞ Host a reception for new graduates following church; recognize all persons in your congregation who are involved in higher education—faculty, staff, administrators.
June	☞ Host a program by a Black College Fund intern in your church.

Resources

General Resources

The following resources can be ordered from the Division of Higher Education, P.O. Box 340007, Nashville, TN 37203-0007; telephone: 615-340-7402 (unless otherwise indicated).

College Bound. A guide to selecting a college, with information about United Methodist schools, colleges, and universities, and loans and scholarships. Free. Quantities of 1-9 are available from the Division of Higher Education. Larger quantities of up to 100 are available in multiplies of 10 from Cokesbury at 800-672-1789, item number 850520.

New Perspectives. A semiannual newsletter for annual conference Boards of Higher Education and Campus Ministry or equivalent structure. Free.

Public Policy Update. A newsletter presenting information on current public policy concerns impacting higher education. Three issues per year. Free.

Handbook for the Annual Conference Board of Higher Education and Campus Ministry. A book of suggestions for the organization of and procedures for this important board of each annual conference (130 pages).

Annual Conference Higher Education Support Data. An annual compilation of annual conference financial support of Campus Ministry, the Black College Fund, Colleges and Universities, and Loans and Scholarships.

Education: The Gift of Hope (Revised). A book for use by congregations and individuals. The resource presents a history of the United Methodist concern for education, a consideration of current issues, and a challenge for congregational involvement in meeting education needs in the community. Available from Cokesbury at 800-672-1789, item number 792047.

Black College Fund

Unless otherwise indicated, resource materials are available through United Methodist Communications at 888-UMC-3242. Please provide the code and quantity needed when calling. Videos may be ordered through EcuFilm at 800-251-4091.

Your Hands. A motivational poster. Free. (Code 771182)

Historically Black Colleges Related to The United Methodist Church.

Location of and brief information about each of the black colleges historically related to The United Methodist Church. Free. (Code 411835)

Offering Envelopes. To be used in interpreting and promoting the Black College Fund. Free. (Code 406452)

Quarterly Report. A financial report showing the Black College Fund apportionment and giving by conferences. Free. Available from the Black College Fund, P.O. Box 340007, Nashville, TN 37203-0007; telephone: 615-340-7378.

Update. A quarterly newsletter with current information about the colleges and the Black College Fund. Free.

Campus Ministry

The following resources can be ordered from the Campus Ministry Section, General Board of Higher Education and Ministry, P.O. Box 340007, Nashville, TN 37203-0007; telephone: 615-340-7404 (unless otherwise indicated).

Campus Ministry: The Church Beyond Itself by Donald G. Shockley (Westminster/John Knox, 1989). An introduction to the history, theology, and present mission of campus ministry in The United Methodist Church. 144 pages. Available from the author. Telephone: 615-661-6464.

So . . . What About God Now That You're Off to College? A six-panel brochure suggesting ways that high school graduating seniors can continue to grow in faith while they are in college.

Orientation. A 48-page magazine for first-year college students. Available each May. For ordering and cost information, contact the Campus Ministry Section.

The Directory of Ministries in Higher Education (annual). A comprehensive listing by state and campus of all United Methodist-related campus ministries and college chaplaincies, support agencies, and organizations. Published each November. Free.

Campus Ministry Matters. Newsletter of the Campus Ministry Section. For campus ministers, college chaplains, annual conference leaders, and other interested persons. Quarterly. Free.

CD Journal. Resource designed to help campus ministries and local congregations form Covenant Discipleship groups for students and faculty on their campuses and in their congregations. Available all year.

Local Church Information Packet. A packet of information about the church's ministries with college students and the United Methodist Student Movement. Available all year. Free.

Schools, Colleges, and Universities

The following resources can be ordered from the Division of Higher Education, General Board of Higher Education and Ministry, P.O. Box 340007, Nashville, TN 37203-0007 (unless otherwise indicated).

Schools, Colleges, and Universities of The United Methodist Church. A complete listing of higher education institutions related to The United Methodist Church. Includes a map of their locations. Free in quantities of 25. Available from Cokesbury, 800-672-1789, order number 740476.

Handbook of United Methodist-Related Schools, Colleges, Universities, and Theological Schools, with a Guide to United Methodist Loans and Scholarships. Provides information about each United Methodist-related institution, charts of the major areas of study at each college and university, and information about United Methodist loans and scholarships. Available from Cokesbury, 800-672-1789, order number 740534.

Directory of the International Association of Methodist-Related Schools, Colleges, and Universities (IAMSCU). Lists 636 institutions, representing 59 nations, related to the World Methodist Council. Free.

Horizons in United Methodist Higher Education Ministries. A one-page newsletter designed and edited to include news from your annual conference as well as from the general church. For details, contact the Office of Annual Conference Relations, Division of Higher Education, 615-340-7402. Free.

Loans and Scholarships

The following resources can be ordered from the Office of Loans and Scholarships, General Board of Higher Education and Ministry, P.O. Box 340007, Nashville, TN 37203-0007 (unless otherwise indicated).

The Loans and Scholarships Resource Kit. Includes a brochure on the United Methodist Loan Program and United Methodist Scholarship Program; Report of Offerings; Scholarship Program flyers; a map and listing of United Methodist-related schools, colleges, and universities; special Sundays materials; and a preliminary United Methodist loan application. The resource kit is designed for the local church ministry team on higher education and campus ministry. The first kit is free.

Student Day Materials. Bulletin inserts and offering envelopes. Available through United Methodist Communications, P.O. Box 1616, Alpharetta, GA 30009-1616; telephone: 888-862-3242.

NOTE: For the most current listing of all resources, please contact the Division of Higher Education, General Board of Higher Education and Ministry, P.O. Box 340007, Nashville, TN 37203-0007.

Places and People Who Offer Further Help

These Guidelines help you know the tasks to be done and provide background information. What if you need information or help not found in the Guidelines?

Your nearby campus minister will be pleased to answer questions or visit your church to help.

Your annual conference Board of Higher Education and Campus Ministry or equivalent structure will know the facts relating to higher educational institutions and campus ministry units in your conference. You can get the name of the chairperson from your pastor.

The church relations officer of the United Methodist colleges or universities in your annual conference can provide more information about those institutions.

The Office of Annual Conference Relations, Division of Higher Education, General Board of Higher Education and Ministry, offers information and publications from a national perspective. You can contact the office at P.O. Box 340007, Nashville, TN 37203-0007; telephone: 615-340-7402.

The United Methodist Foundation for Christian Higher Education, P.O. Box 340005, Nashville, TN 37203-0005; telephone: 615-340-7385.

Discover Resources on the Internet

Find resources and connections for your ministry in higher education on the Internet! The Division of Higher Education has developed several home-pages on the Internet's World Wide Web. These pages provide information about United Methodist-related schools, colleges, universities, theological schools, and campus ministries; loans and scholarships; the Black College Fund; the United Methodist Student Movement; public policy issues; and the United Methodist Foundation.

Check out the Web! Use the information. Send suggestions for additional pages and improvements to Jim Noseworthy, P.O. Box 340007, Nashville, TN 37203-0007; e-mail: jnose@gbhem.org.

Division of Higher Education Web Pages

United Methodist-Related Schools, Colleges, Universities, and Theological Schools, with Links to Institutions' Web Pages
http://www.gbhem.org/schools.html

United Methodist-Related Campus Ministries and Chaplaincies
http://www.gbhem.org/campus.html

United Methodist Loans and Scholarship Programs
http://www.gbhem.org/gbhem/scholar.html

The Black College Fund
http://www.umc.org/benevol/BCF/

On the Move, **the magazine of the UMSM**
http://www.gbhem.org/onthemove/

The United Methodist Student Movement
http://www.umsm.org

Higher Education and Public Policy
http://www.gbhem.org/pubpol.html

The United Methodist Foundation for Christian Higher Education
http://www.umfche.org

Division of Higher Education Home Page
http://www.gbhem.org/highed.html